The Longing of the Optic Nerve

The Longing
of the
Optic Nerve

POEMS BY

LAWRENCE C. GOECKEL

Cover Art: Redon, Odilon (1840-1916). The Eye, Like a Strange Balloon, Mounts toward Infinity. Series: For Edgar Poe, 1882. Private Collection.
Photo Credit: HIP/Art Resource, NY

Cover Design: Kelly Cockrell

Contents

Interior Moonlight

In
the rippled shadow
under the footbridge,
shovel jaw carp lie
motionless in
duckweed

The
honk of migratory
geese lost in low
clouds blankets the
plaintive punctuation
of a distant cuckoo

Arcing
towards the water in a
slow sweep,
exhausted snow cranes
fly in out of the
darkness

A
solitary boatman raises
his hissing lantern
over the lagoon, as if
stalking a lost
memory . . .

Clutched
inside the hushed
rhythm of owl wings,
a limp mouse is
carried deeper into
night

Noon passes by in a train
  pulling a load of red trees--
  the bark half stripped off
An engineer's leather glove
  waves as it goes through
  a town that's nothing
  more than a dime
  under a plate on a lunch counter,
  a white lace curtain fluttering
  in a coal stained home near the highway

A man drops from a boxcar with
  a single complaint against life,
  anthracite sliding from under
  a pair of worn brogans
He heads down the slope towards
  the tree line and then he's gone,
  gone like a sound
The readers waited a long damn time
  for this character,
  afraid the whole thing
  would turn out to just be
  landscape, and now nothing--
  as if the afternoon
  were just a hole in a drive-in screen or
  the last ring of a telephone
  before the caller gives up

On the road drawn
  towards the weave in the sunset--
  a small figure,
  lost hold of before
  the author could put him on paper,
  reemerges, headed west
Behind the shattered cornstalks

left standing after the harvest,
among the unwritten books waiting in
the growth of trees along the
train tracks--
the crickets begin
chewing up the night

Vines   with clusters of white buds   nudge
each other   warp around one another
within our bodies These vines are ligaments
of sleep

Gene Frumkin

Ivy

It's late afternoon at Gene's house,
months after his death, and I'm
watering his lawn while thousands of
books hold up the sale of his home.
"Hey, don't forget to water the ivy," his
neighbor jokes, referring to the strange
vine that has spent years trying to gain
entry to the house, like a starfish trying
to pry open an oyster. I am drawn into
reverie by little white moths flitting over
ivy berries among the shining leaves, as
if something that Gene has left behind, a
remnant of one of his epistemological
proofs — that the past is longer than the
future and unstoppable in its growth. In
the ongoing encounters I have with
Gene in my sleep, he moves freely,
unencumbered by reports of his death
but prevented from wandering too far
by vines which hold him, inversely, to
my dreams. Inside the house, his old
bed still sags in the shape of his sleeping
body.   An electric clock on the
nightstand patiently turns over one
number after another, a rolodex of the
hours. In the silence, the words in his
poems are dusky berries that grew on a
vine all their own, revealing the
relentless form behind his life, as if that
had been their intention all along.

"Don't touch the girls," the bouncer warns. The cashier, disgusted, takes my money and goes back to her crossword puzzle. A tattooed woman gyrates in front of me. She contemptuously points her breasts at my eyes. We share a mutual revulsion and I tip her, finish my beer, and leave.

Another woman hurries past, opens the club door, and disappears inside. A quick sandwich, a phone call, who knows? A bus designed to look like an old streetcar passes by. A garbage truck halfway down the block pours carefully bagged trash into itself. The empty dumpster lid slams shut, desire gone, the evening all but over.

A bluebottle fly deliriously slips
                          back and forth from life to death,
                                          on a red wall.
The leaning ladder does not mystify its purpose:
                          there is always a way out of here.

                              *

An exaggerated landscape with occasional body hairs.
                    Bird, and again bird.   An eyeball
hopping on one leg.
A lot of that.

                              *

Among the growing postulates of lunar geometry,
                    hunger is the space between objects
& the sun a grey/white spider,
cooling off.

                              *

A smeared red line   blows along
a blue beach
                    pursued by black drops of paint
trying to impose order

                              *

Night gropes its way onto the canvas,
                              its stars steadfast on their
strings.   *Glow, little ones,*
          glow.
Joan says, half aloud,   and stands motionless.

                              *

The #2 bristle brush   in his hand dripping
          into a blue pool
in front of   his right foot.

Q. What do flowers longing for insects as they
   waggle their brightly colored sex organs and a
   well-dressed Parisian couple looking coffee
   slopped into cafe saucers have in common?

A: Any two objects can form a pair
   as long as they are together — like a barn
   on its last legs, full of swallows.

Q. Last night, the city's unwashed windows
   were preoccupied with silhouettes of people
   having sex. Does this have any connection
   with the figs coming in, each sagging like a
   testicle in its own sac?

A. Thoughts like these
   will cost you
   your psychic powers.

Q. If the soul departing is a "boxcar full of white
   chickens rolling silently past", how does a
   clockwork of clouds use the Eiffel Tower to
   track the errors of time?

A. Always on schedule, the moment of death
   bulges towards us,
   like the agent of some larger fury.

Odilon Redon's family saw his soul depart as a
loose swarm of gray molecules squeezing out a
drafty window and heading for the sky, before
returning to earth as a meteorite crashing into a
crowded fairground.

> Outside, a perverse wind formed clouds in
> shapes so sensual that villagers were forced
> to keep their children inside. The sky was a
> bad sea that returned every 300 years, last
> documented by Brueghel the Elder.

over the barnyards. An egg hatched in
the Bordeaux with a goose's head on a
snake's body. Bearded fish with pleased
expressions swam through the air over
the village square.

> Wooly spiders, balancing on three legs, slid
> across kitchen floors with drugged smiles
> on their faces. A frightening eye opened on
> the moon. France turned a dingy brown at
> the end of the year.

A young woman gave birth to a small,
older woman. A hot air balloon shaped
like the head of the Virgin Mary, with a
moon shaped infant in its gondola, left
Paris, headed towards the Plains of
Infinity.

> Carp with human lips were pulled out of canals. A
> new Europe, absorbed with mechanical contrivance,
> united behind mornings smelling of stale beer.

The populace fell in love with the plumes of enormous
new smokestacks exhaling into winter skies. Long lines
of steaming villagers, holding lunch pails and clicking
with their tongues, anxiously waited for factory gates to
be assembled.

Women's legs, their sex
exposed to the landscape, are
visible inside an open
boxcar

I nonchalantly look over my
shoulder and walk to the
train

Dropping my shorts, I close
my eyes and thrust myself
into one of the women

Who happens to be my
sleeping wife, who is
unaware

That a perverse relic of the
Second World War has just
rolled in

I return to sleep, allowing
this rare cargo of gardenias
to continue north in the
moonlight

Up the tracks, a drunk
frantically waves his muddy
pink blanket in the train
lantern's light

Certain that he has missed
something very important
and hoping it'll come back
soon

Message from the Fotomat

A bit of aluminum and glass in the middle of asphalt,
  paint blistering in the sun,
  standing unmoved in this very second
  that has taken two billion years to form
The moon streaks across, the stars pop out,
  the drugs wear off
Nothing is to be learned from things beyond
  that which is already known

It is my opinion that when we say goodbye
  it means forever, that stars bring out
  the hidden sickness in the sky
We are fading... hardly here anymore
Our shadows change clothes like
  leaves twittering on weak stems behind us
Something wrong or very golden
  is unwriting us
As we try to photograph it

Photos of a botched sunset
  over a monotonous silver green sea,
  are handed back to us in an envelope
We are a swamp of lost memories
  resurrected by the lies of photographs,
  the wandering odor of sulfur,
  the song of the red winged blackbird,
  cattails fading in the heat

This world wants to eliminate
  the plurality of existence
  dripping like the small air conditioning unit
  hanging from the Fotomat
A rusting roof, walls protected by a yellow curb,
  radio dimly playing inside
This is the best music we have ever heard

After the Fotomat window closes,
  a flag pole chain at the V A hospital
  clangs in the half light
The trash heads north in the wind of the parking lot
A plastic lid with a straw through its center
  wheels along like a one-legged man
  on a unicycle
A bright, dangerous blue
  begins to fill in the shadows

Sparrows fly out of an erupting volcano

The fleeing punctuation of a Pacific sunset

In flight with two mourning doves, the ghost inside the sparrow

Pleased with its gray brown intensity

Sparrows fill with pleasure as the sprinklers come on

Soaking a dead man lying on his lawn

Sparrows eat bread crumbs from the carpet in the lobby of a violent hotel

Flecked with gore, they hop around the junk in the yard, making the junkyard children start to cry

Sparrows dot the pines, patient as prayers

In a religion no one need bother to join

You manage to fall in love. Of course, she was a mannequin before all the elective surgery and your children automatically close their nylon eyelashes whenever you lay them down. Your dining room table is an ironing board and the sound of dishes being put away leaves you feeling full. Television is a fish tank announcing the death of royalty, as the eyes of playing cards weep. But for a while everything has been going great: when you speak at parties the faces of clocks stop ticking to listen. Your jokes send people to the hospital for stitches

Then you come home one day and the kitchen is rattling its weapons. The bathroom is reverting to swamp land. You open the door to your sleeping quarters and apes are hauling your bedding up trees. The family who loves the life you provide them flees. You call 911 and the recording says, "Ah, you complain too much." The cats of course act like nothing is wrong, rolling on their backs, wanting their bellies rubbed.

You leap fences, amazed at your own speed, yet the armed man behind you walks slowly, gaining. A dull witted sheriff's deputy follows you everywhere, asking questions that end in small barred rooms. A desperate newspaper wraps itself around your feet. You wonder at the slow words falling off its pages and let it go. It blows high, wrapping back and forth away from you into the sky.   A blessing.

The sky drops down, breaking off olive branches, destroying the past. A vineyard explodes upward, adding a purple tint to its tornado before falling to earth in tiny abstract pieces.

Things that never fly fill the air: mattresses, espresso machines, pictures of dead relatives, all balling upwards towards daylight, like sardines pursued by a black tip shark.

The landscape waits below with a gondola roosting in the cypress trees. As if it could suppress its sexual longing no more, a broken steeple penetrates the duomo lawn, releasing its swallows.

In Rome, cyclones of people ascend counterclockwise in the wind's upward gravity, screaming as they disappear into clouds.

All the written characters of the ages rise with them, leaving behind the odor of elephants and ragged signs swinging in the wind with their letters ripped off.

A few final birds huddle in cliffs along the Amalfi Coast. The shattered wheat fields of Tuscany feebly wave goodbye, as runaway shards of landscape from the Machine Age finish tearing the sky apart.

Small bubbles headed up to television screens from a submerged car broadcast in a diffuse gold. A beautiful young woman calmly waved at a camera the rescuers had lowered into the river. I drove down to where news camera lights were blinding the surface of the water and, because I cannot remember how one thought leads to the next, jumped in. I touched the passenger door that wouldn't open, cheeks bulging, my hair frantic with effort. She tapped on the window as if to tell me I didn't belong down there. I surfaced for air and dove back down. It was like trying to return to a dream lost in dark water. Impossible.

Though life kept us apart, I occasionally saw her from the morning bus, holding her robe together with one hand while the other picked up a newspaper in a strange yard. Other times, I'd see her using the reflection of the window to put on her lipstick as she passed by my apartment in the bus at night. Out of these chance encounters, we had a child. Evenings, I return home discouraged and sit with my daughter on our blue couch smelling of cigarettes and spearmint gum. We watch *The Undersea World*. "Mr. Cousteau, heee can find her," she says, with her hopefully comic French accent.

After a while, I come to my senses. A car passes by outside with its front end off the ground, dutifully following a tow truck. Behind the apartment, blue lights practice Arabic on the bottom of the swimming pool. A sea tern circles and skims, searching for insects confused by the water's surface. Like her mother, my daughter disappears. As I click through the channels, I briefly see her waving from an island in paradise with a single palm tree. Unable to find my way back to her with the remote, I call out. But my expression of love is as mute as if it were spoken among fish inside an aquarium.

1. Cupped like the invisible ball in the head of the question mark, the moon looks down, chewing thoughtfully. Only a face to start with and that— missing its ears, as if evidence of a violent criminal past. Retired from starring in cowboy movies, while a piano tinkles inside the dance hall— the moon, balanced on a black thread along the horizon, has grown enormous in its solitude.

2. Weary of the traffic light blinking red with nobody waiting, the moon rouses a pygmy owl, legs trailing straight back, off into the dark. I sit up in bed, as if an organ was being stolen from my body, waking me in the middle of an operation. The moon, feigning its innocence, nearly yawns, triggering a lone crop duster to set out— flying low over undulating wheat fields, hunting the leviathan.

A discontented German cleaning lady, one Frau L___, can't understand how anyone who created a place cramped by giant fruit could even speak in complete sentences. "The linen. Clean them. Herr Magritte wants to cover heads," she mocks as she pulls the curtains. The rain of businessmen in bowler hats outside the window continues. "They never hit the ground or begin to sprout. More interesting is the moonlight Rene never noticed, past its expiration date, spilled by drunken guests on the lawn."

She struggles to rid the place of the odor of beached fish that have grown legs to escape poorly painted water. Dusting Magritte's photograph she observes, "Such a womanly little man, holding his cigarette like an embarrassingly small child. Herr Magritte's nudes all had small nipples since he could imagine no other size having an erotic value. Surrealism is an elaborate excuse for impotence."

A minister of state checks his rumpled flesh in the cloak room. His mistress delicately holds a string with two fingers; at the top of the string floats her head. The minister lifts her skirt, revealing an ass dimpled like a golf ball. A brilliant sky of summer gleams in his eye. A group of Belgians rows up the balustrade. Hiding in the maid's room, Frau L____ lights a cigarette and turns on the little black and white set to indulge her secret passion for televised bowling.

She sighs and follows the bell tones downstairs to sign for another delivery of missing landscape. A huge blue ball is parked in the mansion's driveway like a dead rubber sunrise. Red neon, rented by the trustees of the estate to advertise high dollar art, paints the mansion windows. Frau L____ notes with contempt that the businessmen's heads have become all scalp, the front exactly the same as the back. The great lawn is covered with exposed roots holding axes next to stumps that have felled and sold their own trees. The shade has been raked into blackbirds, a great flock that rises over the Seine.

Genesis

The earth was simultaneously infected with enormous anthills and mankind. We ate yams roasted over a fire as birds lingered over the tree line. The air was colored by the velocity of each breeze, the faster the wind, the more the afternoon was tinted by the red/violet end of the spectrum until a permanent sunset flooded back from the dammed horizon. Fruit refused to fall. Trees grew twenty years before releasing a single enormous pear or coconut. Night skies were full of dreamers riding bicycles and gossiping about life on the other continents. Our shadows had lives of their own, running away from us like dogs eager to make contact with their own kind before coming home late, unshaven, strange. Fresh grass grew in our footprints. We walked a long way, until we could see the strings holding the shadows to the trees and knew to call it an evening.

Revelations

A plague of embarrassing facts kept us moving to escape those who knew the details until we were stopped by a horizon of Soviet Bloc apartments. "Welcome to the worker's paradise," I said. A scrap of tent canvas reading, "Behold, He cometh with clouds," flapped in the wind.

Muffled moans of pleasure came from doors opened and suddenly closed along a hundred mile corridor in the heavens. When the storm finished rubbing the blue off of the sky, it chattered off towards the east, leaving behind the smell of burnt insulation. A bonsai covered with spray-on snow was all it left of Japan. An airship broke loose and affectionately nudged its way along the skyscrapers, looking for the past. Watched by binoculars, two employees of the state threw bodies in black bags off the dock. We stood there looking at each other's throats, large and useless, an unstoppable laughter coming from our hands.

On a summer afternoon soon to be lost in the archaeological record, we are still here— little more than animals with lawns: blue grass and fescue dotted by dandelions and an Austrian pine scratching itself in the wind. The whole scene producing only 2 grams of coal 10,000 years from now. A safe place to smoke a couple of numbers.

Next door, a mower coughs into action, disturbing the senility of the lawn. Two tanagers sing from the pines, as if afflicted with human emotion. The roses along the back fence redden like ripe punctuation. Despite my best efforts, we have pigeons. I sneeze and a large bird flies out from the pine, as if part of an illness for which I am the source.

A line of quail pauses on the cinderblock fence and drops one-by-one back into the arroyo. A hummingbird rests on top of a tree stake, then zooms off, too smart to stick around. A pair of victorious sparrows flies in side-by-side, having chased a crow two miles down wind-- as a roadrunner rattles its throat from its nest in the salt cedar.

The leaves on the Russian olive droop as if they've given up but can never die. A 2-inch cigar stub sits on the edge of a rusting iron table, looking like the rest of my life. As daylight retreats, a barn owl, with its human-sized intelligence, begins softly hooting—a satire of the light as it falls from my bedroom window, searching for loose change in the lawn.

Noircolepsy

Night reflects the diner back onto itself: the cash register on its perch, the pencil behind the waitress' ear, the ticket holder as it spins towards a Swede with an enlarged heart, sweating in the kitchen

An obese diner asks for another pat of butter for his roll   A baked chicken steams in front of him, next to mashed potatoes with white gravy and green peas

A clown in white face sulks over his coffee cup until he is interrupted by a fork dropped on a plate Smoke lingers over his booth from a red lip-stained cigarette held in a gloved hand

The diners furtively watch him, as if they know they are figures in a dream, whose murders he cannot be held accountable for once he awakes

The clown stares at the brown Os left by generations of sloppy coffee drinkers on his table top   The second hand stutters forward   "Just get out," he whispers

One by one, this aggregate of thieves, unemployed musicians, and sleepwalkers leaves their unfinished meals and slips back into the darkness

"The truly crazy are always the calmest," he says to himself and lifts two fingers, listlessly signaling the tomato sauce stain on the waitress's white uniform for a refill of coffee

The kitchen is silent, except for the crackle of tobacco burning in a cigarette in the corner of the Swede's mouth

Inside the diner's rapidly rotating ceiling fan, an illusory set of blades slowly moves in the opposite direction, as if part of a slower, much older, night

She was quick with the keys to her place   I bent down a corner of the venetian blinds, dead leaves huddled on the balcony as if they didn't want to be seen

I felt like I'd committed a crime in my sleep   "I ain't got much hope," I said   "I know," she said   "Why don't you stop all that writing crap, and start paying attention to me?"

Looking at the chipped paint on her toenails, I knew that wasn't going to happen   She worked some place in her underwear and men paid a lot to buy her drinks

"Why don't you get another job?" I asked   "Listen," she said   "there are two things I know how to do: to smoke and to excite men."

The match she held to her cigarette went out, having thought its one thought   "We should get started," I said

She reached both hands around for the clasp on her bra, closing one eye to avoid the smoke coming from the cigarette in her mouth

As she undressed, I imagined knifing the man she worked for, not for love or to join a navy of fugitive pimp killers, but for the way he licked chicken grease from his fingers

I tried to say something hopeful, but there was a syringe in the bathroom cup next to her toothbrush and pictures of handsome men from newspapers were taped on the wall

I wasn't sure how I fit into that picture   The gin
numbed me like a religion, a religion that I enjoyed

I slid back into the hallway before dawn and headed
downstairs to look for a taxi Outside, the whole damn
street was an eraser smear

The words on the realtor sign were no longer legible
And the black weeds growing out of pores in the
vacant lots, retreated back into the shadows

The landlady found him this morning   before   the
swimming pools opened their eyes   Sprinklers hissing as
the city runs dry   Found him halfway in the ice box, as if
the body crawled by itself, seeking refrigeration   The jaw
of the corpse sticking out, disputing the facts   In a
delirium straight out of chain smoking Latin American
literature   The corners where the white walls meet the
ceiling, hairy with shadow

The best of me is missing to a hangover   I feel like a
painting with the eyes cut out   I look through the dead
guy's crap for the hell of it, using a pencil to dump a few
things with nothing to do with the crime into plastic bags
"Death exposes what we spend our lives trying to conceal,"
I tell a couple of rookies   All of the other old timers are off
today, drinking vodka tonics or fucking someone else's
wife, working on books where the characters are all dead
and the writer's trying to interest readers in the layout of
the furniture

The body's just a bookmark for a shipyard cook who's going
to lose a few nights of watching television   A cheap
detective novel folded between pages 73 and 74, where the
cops talk like this:

> Life starts with a few words on a
> birth certificate. Then there's a
> lot of paperwork. Right before
> someone's name gets carved on
> a tombstone, I get called in
> to figure out what went wrong . . .

A pile of bills that won't get paid anytime soon sits on the
back of the couch, tossed into a hat   Everything is
permanently unfinished, except for the redhead from the
escort agency he called last night, sitting on the couch with

a high heel dangling off of her left foot, offering her boredom as an alibi ever since she got picked up this morning

A cop in the kitchen encroaches on the nothingness the victim has created for himself, holding a dead arm up and looking at the wrist watch   Another examines an errant hair growing from the dead man's ear   "The victim woke up and found the redhead helping herself to his wallet," I write   "Gut shot with his own gun in the ensuing struggle."   I flip my notebook closed with great drama and step outside

A dog yawns on the lawn   The wind pushes the leaves into a new pattern on the sidewalk   The six on the door is really a nine hanging by its foot from a nail   Reporters and cops stand around the yard like there's a party inside The redhead comes out with a jacket wrapped around her head, on the way to an unseen cruiser   They've wrapped the other evidence in plastic and put it in the trunk   A pair of size twelve feet sticking out from a gurney sheet is all the public gets to see   The cop cars move away slowly, as if hoping somebody will break from a building and run for it

The city lights wash out the sky, leaving a few worn out stars that nobody bothers to look at anymore   As I sit in my unmarked car, I see the police helicopter beacon a quarter mile to the east, scattering a herd of white goats in Topanga canyon   I back out of the driveway   A shudder moves across the valley   The neighborhood fades into movie screen blue

I hit the brakes. Two boys on the overpass hurl a cinderblock at my windshield. Pieces of my side mirror lie scattered on the road behind me.

The windshield is still whole. The engine is purring. Heat is coming off the metal floor and the parkway is quiet, as if nothing has happened.

I put it in reverse and back up the on ramp, hoping to chase the kids down the sidewalk in my truck. At the top of the ramp, I see a helicopter

Two blocks away, spotlighting a convenience store surrounded by boys. A Korean storeowner has chased a shoplifter out into the street and is getting beaten

With his own mop. Barely able to stand, he makes it inside and locks his door. The boys who beat him, blink uncomfortably in the spotlight

Then run down the street, crazily waving their arms. The beam switches off. I return to Suitland Parkway and drive-- until my truck disappears back into the dark.

I keep looking upwards, knowing that the helicopter is still out there, combing a spotlight through the city where I live, persistent as God himself, unable

To permanently change anyone's behavior, yet, finding satisfaction in expressions of foolish guilt as humanity looks towards a watchful sky.

Through the fonduq's window the sun bleaches the last trace of red out of the landscape. The city is busy between its silences, preparing the evening. Men twirl their prayer beads outside domino halls. Women in burkas move their black blots from place to place. Water gurgles through the pipes in our walls. Just as we fall asleep there is the sharp ting of overheated boulders cooling in the desert.

The next morning we walk through walled lanes smelling of mint tea. Two former criminals, maimed according to the law, sit on a bench near the Nazarene beauty parlor. The song of the muezzin blankets hillsides from the minarets. We catch a ride on a produce truck out to where olive trees are manicured along intricate irrigation channels.

The report of an ancient cannon severs the afternoon. We walk back to the town square to watch the religious parade. A prisoner's blindfold is removed as he is forced to kneel in front of a hooded man with both hands on the handle of a curved sword, its tip point down. I look towards the sky, towards the clouds behind the glare of the central mosque, hoping for intervention.

"The evil inside him knows it is about to die," My husband says. I reach for his arm but he grabs my hand and says, "Wait. It's my turn to see something interesting". His eyes are eager, a sweat of animal excitement on his face. I pull away as the condemned man's heart sprays its blood through the severed neck.   I struggle through faces, back towards the hotel.

I wanted to travel to a place where the world is not ruined by our understanding of it.   Where the literal holds sway during long, paralyzed afternoons. Where, as they say, *The sleep of the body is the waking of the spirit.*   I collapse into bed. The ceiling fan rotates so slowly it seems to be in collusion with the heat. I am drenched in a deep sleep. Do not even hear my husband enter from the late afternoon.

After midnight, I leave his rhythmic breathing in our darkened room and walk through deserted streets, staying in the shadows as if a ghost of a lower order. This city plastered in white mud swells up, eager to be seen in moonlight. The boulders out in the desert are constantly unburied and reburied as the wind rehearses its strategies for destruction of any town foolish enough to exist here.

I sit a long time, cooled by the low breezes that hold to the curvature of the planet, listening to big trucks shifting gears out on the moonlit highway. I walk back, open the door to our room and stand in front of the bathroom mirror for several seconds before my face recognizes me. I retch several times. Nothing. I pull the toilet chain and climb back into bed, hoping for the erasure of sleep among the fine particles of sand permanently lodged between the fonduq's bed sheets.

*In Budapest, you become the things that are
moving towards you.*

Along the Danube, seagulls are
drinking from potholes. The 7:19 bullies a
crushed Lada down the tracks as a cleaning
crew calmly passes through high rise office
windows. In the apartment building next
door, a woman warms herself in front of the
kitchen stove.

The ticket windows are closed and all
the trains have left. A helpful man in a
jogging suit and gold chains, his voice in
need of a shave, asks me, "Hey man, you
like pretty ladies? Come on man. It's the
best." "I just need a ride," I tell him. "Okay,
I'll get you a ride," he says, and leads me
into the parking lot.

The door of a badly damaged Lada
kicks open. A woman is lying across the
back seat without clothes on. Under the
short hairs, something winks at me. I hand
him 50 kroner from my wallet to get a better
look.

I stop a cop and ask for directions.
He yawns, lights a cigarette, asks me for
drugs, and then points to a bus waiting at
the curb. It's full of travelers without
suitcases going to the airport. A man is
sleeping in the luggage rack. I sit behind the
driver.

"Thanks for stopping, but I'm out of
money," I say. "That's okay, I always stop

here. But, be careful," he warns, with a jerk of his head towards the back of the bus. "These are not good people." "Maybe somebody better will get on," I say. "Not with them in here," he says. "You look familiar," I tell him. "I gave you a ride last week. Same place, same time of night. We had the same conversation."

I get off the bus, go upstairs to my flat, and wake up on the couch with my hat still on. My girlfriend comes home from her cleaning job and leaves her clothes on the kitchen floor. Her left hand holds her hair back as she lights a cigarette from the burner and then stands in front of the stove, warming herself. She is more comfortable without clothes on than any woman I've ever seen.

She knows this is the reason I'm still here. Her clairvoyance makes truth a senseless limitation. "Do you want to take the bed for a ride?" she asks. I go back over to the television: the Danube has become so polluted, seagulls are being filmed drinking from potholes. I turn it off.

From the bedroom window, I look down on the train station parking lot, deserted now, except for a crushed Lada and a man in a jogging suit with gold chains. I shut the blinds, leaving it for another day, and climb on top of her.

My Dear Herr Doppelganger

I found my daughter on the daycare playground and told her she could play while I called her mother

A strangely familiar voice answered the phone, continuing the conversation it was having for several minutes before answering me

I asked him for my wife   She got on the phone and became very distressed as she told me my daughter had already come home with me

I once again spoke to a man's voice more like mine than my own This time he told me he was planning a trip to the ocean for my wife and her family

I told him that this was proof he wasn't me   I would never be so generous   He asked me to help with the arrangements

I hung up the phone and ran to the daycare playground   My daughter was gone   There were only boys wearing long plastic monster fingernails

They were depressed because there were no other children willing to act scared of them   I began running, one of the monster boys chasing me

I was relieved when I arrived home to find out I wasn't already there   Less fortunate to find nothing was as I remembered

My wife was more beautiful, but several inches shorter   A clock left at the dump years ago was on the wall

Tiny deer hung by their feet in the refrigerator   All props, to prevent me from finding my way back   All disturbingly comfortable

My double would claim the world that I was already forgetting, leaving smug faces on the family portraits   Outside I heard someone cracking around in the branches

A horrible laughter began coming from the trees   And all of these damned people, passing in cars, waved as if they knew me

A group of strangers waits for
the bus, all looking down the
street at the same moment for
something that will carry them
into the future, and one of them
takes his shirt off, as if to say:
this is my city and this is how I
live, while smoking the last
cigarette from a pack, now lying
crumpled at his feet as an
asthmatic grandmother stands
with two small children, trying
to avoid the smoke, while a
stoned and anxious teenager
with a quarter turn to his ball
cap, considers walking to the
next bus stop but just then the
bus appears, blocking the view,
and, with a puff of exhaust,
leaves behind an empty bench,
along with the feeling that if
there was something we should
do, we have forgotten what it
was, as arms and hands at the
carwash, just a block away, wipe
water off windshields and the
car fenders sparkle in clean
sunlight.

" . . .waiting for a door in the East River to open to a room full of opium and steam heat."

Ginsberg, HOWL

HOT L

Black fire escape. A bathroom sink lying in the living room. Tenants too fucked up to use the phone. The rooftop E goes out. The other red letters start frantically flashing— "HOT L, HOT L, HOT L".

Outside, dockworkers sleep off lunch on abandoned tires in the park. A sidewalk elm stands on one leg, unable to escape its daily dose of dog urine. While skyscrapers waver in the heat, HOT L stands solid.

A woman's bloody scream complicates the smell of cooking trapped on the fifth floor. A door opens only as far as the chain will allow. An eyeball watches the security mirror at the end of the hallway.

A tenant dials 911. When the operator asks for the address the caller panics and hangs up. The beat cop knows the scene: five hot floors up, broken elevator, no body, no eyewitnesses.

A police siren drifts past. A faint breeze fights its way through the steam over the East River with a message for everyone too stoned to live anywhere else. The news is not good: "HOT L, HOT L."

It was something my father caught during a tour of Rome, when the lights went out in the catacombs with thousands of corpses on the shelves around him in the echoing darkness. After that, there was one dream inside him that was more intoxicating than the others. In his sleep, he was back underground in Rome, listening to the faint rumble as tour buses pulled in and gypsy hawkers tried to sell the passengers bottled water. When guides brought tourists through his dream, the lights clicked on at the far end of the catacomb like a television at the end of a long tunnel with its sound off. When the tourists left, he shared the dreams of the devout in a narcotic darkness.

Once he crossed paths with this dream, he'd sleep for days. Then he'd wake up just like normal, drive the car to the supermarket, buy meat that was on sale, and put it in the freezer chest in the garage. We had doctors measure his brain waves and test his galvanic skin response. We even hired a psychiatrist to help unravel the power of whatever had hold of him. Dad claimed he couldn't remember any details. The doctor told the family he was guarding his dream.

His waking periods became more troublesome. He'd get out of bed and, without talking or even looking at us, go to the garage, begin sawing and hammering, and by late afternoon we'd have a condominium of bird houses on a steel pole in the backyard. Then he'd go back to sleep and we'd have to turn him so he didn't get bedsores. Several times he sleepwalked out of his room and began looking through every book in the house, as if desperate for a clue to take back with him. He read furiously through cookbooks or motorcycle repair manuals, it didn't seem to matter.

"Think of the money you'll save on burial costs," he told my mother during one of his expeditions into the waking world. Then, true to his word, he disappeared. All that was left of him was an unnaturally warm spot in his bed. We called the police. But no one reported seeing a middle aged man in his pajamas. I'll admit being bothered by his last words to me: "Dreams of the living," he said, "are the imperfect remains of the dead." He was an expert on ancient death. I was always satisfied with simpler things-- like the scent of the desert air as the sprinklers spray the city park across the street and how, as each day ends, we are all that's left of us.

The Platoon Moves Cautiously Into the Village

Slipping outside, he lights a cigarette   A Vietnamese family sleeps on a vinyl covered platform beside their fruit stand   Construction workers, waiting for daylight, rest on blankets along the main street   Several old buildings have been hauled off piece by piece   Tiny scrap fires burn in their pits   Two young women, watching television in a turquoise rooftop apartment, laugh so hard that something must be wrong with them

Old women with bruised faces look for a last chance to pimp underage girls waiting in secret rooms inside the open market   Behind a souvenir store's metal shutters, dolls covered with dust watch over illegal currency exchanges Illuminated air, thick with the night sweats of irrigated fields, surrounds the huge hand painted marquees lining the roof of the all-night theater on the hill   Someday the communists will preserve the movie house as a palace of testimony where local girls can tell what Americans did to them and how revolution has set them free   But tonight, the movies continue their uninterrupted passage, theater patrons nodding under the projector's single beam

He walks back, paralleling moonlit fields where the rice is heavy on its stalks and a train can be heard clattering out of town   Stepping through the courtyard gate, he avoids the neighbor girl's tricycle abandoned for the night   Inside the beaded doorway, all that can be seen of his sleeping companion are her bare legs   He lies beside her, waiting for the fan to blow back over them, as he listens to two rats fighting and running over the ceiling tiles   In another room across the alleys, the night is not passing so easily   Little perfume bottles are being smashed on the floor   A woman is screaming in bad English   "Get out! Go sleep with her if you like to fuck her so much!   Get out!"

rendering the flies silent with its dry buzz. From my window, only an occasional tourist is visible under an unbearable sky. The others stay in shadow-- watching from the cool interiors of mud brick homes. The heat has become a well lit stage, the foreigners out in it— novice actors, trying to

fight off noisy insects in their ears. In Northern Africa, the phones are always broken, the soldiers out of garrison. The acquaintances a traveler was supposed to stay with have just died, or left months ago. Foreigners find they have wandered into a place which values vengeance more than

the hidden cash they carry. The locals live slowly, protected by monotony. What is frequently mistaken for love here is merely patience. Light blows off the brilliant bay, carrying the unfortunate stench of sewage back into the village as if the seawater were befouling the air with our own

comments. Barracuda hide in the glitter of the waves. A fish leapt into a tourist's face last week, overexcited by the sparkle of her

earrings.   When my wife left, so
disappointed, her luggage waiting
for us to get it over with, she must
have seen what was coming, the
desert spreading

inside of us. The heat is all that's left
of the depot with its flowering of
people coming and going. No one
looking out the train windows
anymore

is the face of love I am stuck with.

The detective novel "must punish the criminal in one way or another, not necessarily by operation of the law."
Raymond Chandler

The pain in my right side had exhausted what was left of me The doctors, if you could call them that, couldn't figure it out According to the blood work, I was healthy   Had been for years   But in my dreams, I was burying a body

Finally the doctors said they'd go in   On the morning of the surgery my wife delivered me to a fat woman with soft hands She shaved my belly, then my chest   "That's how I like my men" the nurse said as I went under

A bright blue pain emanated from my midsection   I was in a white bed with a long white curtain around me   It was blinding   A doctor who I'd never seen before said, "We're going to have to go back in   We didn't get it all   Go back to sleep"

I stared down at my abdomen   The 6 inch incision looked like a tightly closed mouth with black bristles sticking out of it   A sheriff's deputy sat in a chair just outside the room, reading a celebrity tabloid

A phony three quarter moon pressed against the black window   The doctor nodded towards the door and whispered, "The cyst we removed contained human remains, some hair, a couple of teeth"

I felt like I was trapped in an Edward Hopper painting   The way the deputy kept reading his paper told me there were going to be a lot of questions

After the third operation, something inside me packed its bags and headed for the highway   I felt like the surgery had exposed a forbidden landscape and the cop was there to prevent the scenery from leaving my body

My wife brought vanilla ice cream; it tasted dishonest   I got out a week later   We glided through town in our freshly waxed car   The sidewalks along our street were lined with balding palms raised like the soft hands of idiots

A tree in our backyard left figs, red inside like children, lying around under its branches   There was a smoky smell to the rose bushes   A helmeted mother and her wobbly daughter rode by on bicycles, waving

Next door, a near sighted man with a fat wife cleaned the leaves from his rain gutters   A milk colored weather balloon from the naval observatory zigzagged across the sky and disappeared into the clouds

But the dog stayed away, as if it could smell prison on my clothes   I watched the light sweat on my wife's upper lip and lit her cigarettes   She was a dream of a woman   Everywhere I went in the house, she was there

I stood on the back porch looking over fields towards the highway   I saw something like clothes shining as they walked west after midnight   I packed a bag and left, following the boulevard at a distance

Where the left turn arrow had worn off the asphalt, I went right   Crunching bits of broken windshield underfoot, I walked slowly up the highway entrance ramp towards a freeway necklace of headlights

I couldn't see the faces inside the cars, but I knew one was coming for me   The window rolled down   Lit by dash light, the deputy's voice said, "Get in   You're going back to the hospital   We're not done"

There is only a spiritual world; what we call the physical world is the evil in the spiritual one.   F. Kafka

Under the Fig Tree

As if devouring the flesh of sinners, wrens and sparrows have ripped into the figs, leaving my tree a series of open wounds. Satan appears in the backyard, pulling damaged figs through his gums and flinging their skins over the fence. Songbirds flutter about him, anxious to whisper in his ear. Sated, he sprawls beside me on the couch, his tongue flicking out, checking the air for scent.

Watching the paternity tests of angry spouses on daytime television, he boasts of his plan to leave all the girls in town impregnated on the same night, overwhelming the hospitals in 9 months with a flood of immaculate conceptions. *But not one of them a Messiah. Like a lottery without a winning ticket. Something to roust His Holiness out of his slumber,* he wheezes.

During the local news Old Scratch suffers a seizure, changing form a dozen times. When the tremors stop, he's stuck again in his homeless incarnation, rambling at full speed. He announces the weather forecast a second and a half ahead of the meteorologist and when we head out for an early evening walk, he stoops to sniff under the cabbage leaves in a neighbor's garden.

When he pauses in the plaza, a storm of pigeons circles counterclockwise overhead before suddenly shooting back into the air: a black and white vortex ascending into a grey sky. Satan disappears with them. I instinctively check my pockets for my wallet and keys. As I walk home, whole trees of roosting finches take off as I pass by.

The next morning wind hatches dead patches on the lawn. The fig leaves blow like green flags at the end of knuckled stems. A cardinal stares inside with supernatural concentration before leaving a smear of fig seeds on the windowsill. I pray that Satan has moved on to another world, but realize there's not a chance. As the prophet says, "If there is another world, it is this one."

Running through the infrared, white figures on a 6″ by 6″ screen get turned into smears on the ground as our plane lands with the gun tapes recording a country none of us sees, without mountains or seashore, its sky— a gray mascara waiting to be wiped off

The stars shine behind me as I leave the air base, passing Italian families as they stroll through their village, stopping to eat gelato al limon with tiny spoons   Inside the café, two deaf old men are playing checkers on a small square table

I sit in a booth to smoke a couple of cigarettes, watching two workers still in their blue coveralls, reflected by a mirror, its edges eaten away by rust   A pasta with some sort of cream sauce sits in front of one of them, growing cold

They occasionally look over their shoulders to make sure I don't understand Italian   The more we need these damn people as friends, the more they reject us, driving circles around soccer stadiums, honking the horns in their little cars, protesting the air war being launched from their country

The waitress moves slowly, as if she must fully imagine each action before she acts   I listen to the slurping of the espresso machine and wonder about the cleanliness of the white towel she uses to wipe the steam stem   I finish my coffee, put out my cigarette, and walk back to the base

The planes are still taking off, leaving tanks caught maneuvering in the mud with perfect holes, like a hot cigar stuck in a bar of soft butter   Not qualified to be our enemies, just our targets, the Serbs sleep on open ground, away from their guns and armament

During the day they roll dead bodies, wrapped in blankets, into fresh trenches or leave them to rot, jaws jutted out   Starved dogs sniff around them, an old urge rising in their bones   The crows are less restrained

The grass has been trampled into dirt outside our mailroom   The temporary roads we have plowed into the hayfields smell of mildewed canvas   The night is running long   The tents along the flightline are snoring   I open a flap and disappear inside one of them of love during another war, one where he is still alive— the quarter moon cratered by the long term effects of alcohol and nicotine. A beautiful woman waits down the street, under a gin sick sky, pushing a lock of hair from her forehead, a basket of laundry in one arm. A storm of Allied planes circles the bombed cupolas, their 50-caliber fire sweeping the Via Veneto like hail.

Undaunted, this barefoot woman calmly sells her roses in the cafes and bodegas of the dead man's dreams. Wheezing, he helps push her cart towards the wreckage of her home. She vanishes as the stars blink on and off from the unstable voltage. Unable to remember which house is hers, he pounds on doors left standing in front of rubble, looking for a place to hide from his death.

A bus load of school children bumps down the cratered road, its haughty yellow the only color outside the gray scale of smoldering buildings. Her nine-year-old face joins the others, sticking her tongue out at him. He finds a shovel with a broken handle and begins digging. But, each time he turns his spade over, dandelions wiggle up, their optimistic yellow flowers preventing him from finishing his own grave.

The unique and supreme pleasure of making
love lies in the certitude of doing evil
                    Charles Baudelaire

                                The
alleyway in front of her apartment
had a memory —   smelling of
Spanish cigarettes, a memory of the
cobbled sound of gloved hands
applauding   gypsies   with   a
balancing goat   "You must leave.
I have grown allergic to just 1/2 the
bed," she'd tell her patrons
while her aged father slept in front
of a window,   dreaming of the
time   the zeppelins bombed
Paris

                                Her
exquisite flesh was perfumed
by the scent of cut flowers, the first
few drops of rain,   and the sun
squeezed into   an orange spot
over violet haystacks Frenchette's
stockinged   legs   descending
from the third floor   inspired
longing at a hundred meters Her
quick glance   from under the
awning   of the Café de Flore
caused   an   immediate   loss   of
memory in married men
                        For her--
sailors ran their ships aground to
wander drunk in the Quartier des
Oubliettes   and   enormous
foreigners   walked tiny dogs on
long   leashes,   asking   questions

Parisians pretended not to
understand   The   homosexuals
in the Rue de Bonaparte were
swept into a fever of imitating her
                              Bakers
paused to watch her pass, and then
resumed scenting the air   with
the smell of long loaves   of
bread Frenchette was the neon at
alley's end, where men with
beautiful wives   prowled for
working girls   pulling up their
garters by the last station of the
Metro She spoke with the most
precise of tongues to souls enslaved
by the promise of pleasure
                           Frenchette
abhorred open space, preferring
narrow streets with lampposts
shedding handbills like leaves,
streets   where the subterranean
clamminess of the Metro was
relieved by the warm, polluted
night-- where the boulevard
whispered to second story
shadows being bent over beds
                        While   her
father ate in lamplight, crumbs
falling into his lap, the pigeons on
her window cooed Drunk on gin,
she placed black tape over her
nipples and curtly addressed
the postcard photographer as he
shot a special remembrance for her
patrons Local admirers took turns
watching through a key hole
as she combed her beautiful thick
pubic hair

Frenchette
married,   dabbed champagne
from her bodice, and continued
lying on the telephone with the
same slight smile as before, until
her husband came home one night
and her hair was red,   a wrong
red Frenchette gave him her hand
to be kissed, whispering, "Ah, my
captor"   and put on her
coat as a limousine waited outside
the apartment, its parking lights
staring up at her window As her
foot alit on the pavement the city's
searchlights, long abandoned,
resumed carving tunnels into the
night

The lightning takes several minutes to leap from one cloud to the next. A burning Ferris wheel spins slowly in the unlit park across from The Farolito. Inside, I sit at the bar beside a Mexican road crew black with asphalt. I turn to listen to the gunfire coming from under the bridge and see myself drinking in a booth, thirty years younger. A woman sits on my young lap, feeling for my wallet. Her tube top covers the scars where the cheap implants went in. A knotted string of words sticks in my throat like a rope disappearing into a well.

I could tell this kid something, but what, that *there is no trap so deadly as the one you set for yourself*? I stagger towards the back, the bathroom walls dotted with hypodermic blood. My mirrored face looks like dried mud. The upholstered bar door swings behind me as I reenter an old city ruined by starlight. In a well-lit stand in the plaza, boys paint nightmares on neckties. On the bridge, a set of arms and legs folds up like a seat in a darkened theater. When I wake up in El Paso, the sparrows are screaming their heads off in the palm trees.

Thirty years from now, the kid at the bar will spend the night in this same hotel room. He'll smoke a cigarette on the edge of the bed as *the city darkens with something more than night.* Counting the change on the dresser twice, he'll pocket a couple of bills and head into Juarez. He'll watch a young man that looks like him drinking in one of the booths with a woman sitting on his lap, feeling for his wallet. Staggering outside, he'll slowly fall on the sidewalk. The last thing he'll ever see is the slow lightning leaping between clouds, as the ranchera music continues to cut off, each time the bar's upholstered doors swing shut.

A blood stain is still visible in the back seat. Palms sweating on the steering wheel, constantly adjusting the rear view mirror, I wave to my downstairs neighbor passing in his car. Back inside the apartment, I feel like a red brick building painted black.

A thunderstorm kills the power without issuing a single drop of rain. My phone rings in the dark. An old woman, confused by the weather, keeps dialing a number that connects her to me.

One of my neighbors, trapped inside the freight elevator, desperately pushes the alarm. The bell dies slowly as the battery drains. Then the damn phone starts ringing again.

When the power comes back on, my heart slows. The rhythmic snoring of an aged neighbor floats through the curtains on a light breeze. I fall asleep and see the toe of a mulched high heel sticking out of a flower bed.

I go outside with a flashlight and check the dirt around the apartment building. But there are only little red leaves, unfurling like boiled hands, as the rose bushes start another season.

Variations

Murder Tattoo

> **Resident of the State of Kansas**: He was once
> just a sly smile hiding in her closet, watching her
> as she slept. His mother felt like a small town
> besieged by lightning, hoping
> he would leave on his own,
> certain he'd keep coming back.

Murder Tattoo

> **Composite Sketch**: Stares
> like a fist hole in drywall.
> Troubling as a match struck inside
> a darkened car in an unlit parking lot.
> Jurors generally afraid
> to look at his face. . .

Murder Tattoo

> **Time Stutters and Slows**: Betrayed
> by one muddy shoeprint
> and wanting nothing
> more complex than revenge
> 3,000 days of bunk, toilet, mirror, sink,
> Bunk, toilet, sink, mirror.

Murder Tattoo

> **Religious Reflection**: On parole, riding
> a kid's bicycle on the sidewalk.
> Sees another man with murder teardrops

71

riding a bike on the other side of the street.
Keeps riding, as if waiting for He
whose face is covered with teardrops.

Murder Tattoo

Unsuspecting Landlady: Before her disappearance
he was last seen throwing a dead snake into the
weeds.
His wheeze-like laughter can still be heard
in the boardinghouse hallway.
They say he handed the glass eye they gave him
in prison back to the parole board.

Murder Tattoo

A New Friend: "I was crazy until a minute ago,"
he laughs, as he sits next to you at the bar.
Then you see the teardrops
under his left eye and the other tattoos
looking as if they crawled up
his neck for a better view of your face.

Although I am dead, my soul shuffles towards a phone that has never rung before, because there are no phones in the afterlife and even if there were, the dead wouldn't answer them.

It's my former wife, surrounded by candles and billing herself as Madam M_____, the clairvoyant. She's contacting the dead from her fortuneteller's parlor to impress a client.

Dying has only worsened my knowledge of death, I say and hang up the phone. I can still hear her. So, I disconnect the cord. But her voice comes through the ventilator. She has *utility bills to pay, a house full of cats to feed . . .*

Flickering, she appears in the windows of eternity, mouth moving without words. The doorbell rings but no one is there, just her eye peering up through the sink drain. This goes on for years.

When her death finally comes, I hear a candle being knocked over and see her cats scrambling, chased by a bouquet of flame.

I sense her presence passing silently by — a faint odor of smoke trailing through a moonlit door and out into a barren landscape where the crude production values of eternity are projecting a desert train off in the distance — soundless, blurred, and then gone.

A   dust
storm snaps off   telephone poles   as it
speeds towards me   a thousand feet high
and pissed off   beyond all reason
                                   I   take
shelter   inside a restaurant   full of elderly
diners   patiently pushing   navy beans
around their plates
                          Outside, a state
fair's   worth of cowboy hats   whips past
chased by a flood   of rice paper parasols
                             When   the
wind stops   I wander back out into   the
darkened parking lot   looking for
more artifacts   spilled over   from the past
                          Human
silhouettes with animal heads   chase each
other   along the ridgeline   in a murderous
pantomime
                             The   solar
apparatus   from a grade school visit
to the planetarium   kicks into motion
with the wailing   of a worn fan belt
                          The   oldest
woman   in the diner   believing herself
to be my wife appears   in the doorway
yelling "Come finish your soup"
                          A pair of
headlights   moves   along the abandoned
highway   without a vehicle
                             As I linger
transfixed by the forgotten music   of a
circus   buried   at four in the morning
rising from beneath my feet

-1-

Shoulder holster slung over his chair, a weary homicide detective sits in his office trying to explain how he ran over a last minute shopper with his arms full of Christmas presents, during pursuit of a shopping mall robbery suspect. With each typewriter clack, the story takes shape. A wreathed door explodes outward from a SWAT team concussion grenade. Christmas ornaments and wrapping paper spew into the street. A nativity scene scatters, as ashes muffle down like snow.

-2-

Standing in front of the television, scratching an infected vein with a steak knife and watching Jimmy Stewart trying to save the family bank, a local man walks over to pull the duct tape off his wife's mouth and says, *I almost forgot. Merry Christmas.* Knowing that the bitchy sheen in her voice is coming back as soon as she can call the cops, he's ripped the phone from the wall and stands there smiling, in charge of this sweetly short-lived, holiday moment.

-3-

While his ex-fiancé's family is singing at candlelight service, he's in a ski mask unsuccessfully searching through their gifts for the expensive necklace he gave her.

Frustrated, he sticks their Christmas tree in the back of his truck, lights it on fire, and throws its tinseled ass off an old suspension bridge. It lies burning on top of the frozen river, as the pines along the banks move their cold branches side to side, imitating the wind. This is, perhaps, his best Christmas ever.

A summer night green with humidity drifts over rooftops. Northern flying squirrels nest in the oak trees. A station wagon rolls past, asking if anyone has seen a lost dog.

Our neighbor pulls his finned Buick into his driveway, gets up on the roof, and drunkenly adjusts the antenna to pick up CBS out of Dayton. A cat silently crosses the street.

My little sister is already asleep, next to a fashion magazine she has torn her favorite pages from to chew on, as her crib mattress warms with her sleeping body.

* * * * *

Forty-six years later, we pour my sister's remains— two middle aged men trying not to breathe in a plume of dust from a black vinyl bag, into urns for her children.

Her husband gracelessly sweeps spilled ash out of the garage. I return to the past: my little sister running down the driveway towards the camera with a red tint still alive in her hair.

The spring smell of wild onions bulbs out of the lawn as a necklace of crows struggles against the wind, calling over their shoulders, sure that the ones behind them will be coming along soon.

The Western, After Hours

"Need I repeat, we have come
without sleep from Nuevo Laredo."

Ed Dorn, *Gunslinger*

1.

Got up in the middle of the night and heard my own voice speaking outside, using words I didn't understand, as if it was having a dream of its own. I looked out the back door and didn't see anything except a pair of sheets out there flapping on the line. Next day my wife said, "You were sleepwalking last night, banging into walls and knocking shit over in the kitchen." When I got out of bed I remembered she'd left months ago, took the kids with her. The kitchen table covered with beer cans and lone toothbrush in a blue enamel cup beside the sink proved it. Of all the fucked-up worlds way off the Interstate, this one turns out to be the real one.

2.

Later that morning, I'm driving the county road into Johnson City when a goddamn African Oryx in the middle of the highway stops my truck. A head ready for somebody's den wall-- three foot spiral horns and a black and white muzzle, is nonchalantly chewing something in the back of its mouth and looking at me through the windshield. I'm a good mile and a half outside the 12-foot fences of the Benson Exotic Preserve, where oryx are on the shooting menu for 4,000 dollars. Looking back at him through the windshield, I feel like I should be on some kind of medication. He confidently bounds off towards the tree line as if to say, *Well, there's nothing wrong with me.* I sit there for a second and then I say out loud, as a warning to myself, "The wife and kids are gone and the oryx are moving in."

I hit the ground so hard I see a white sky with black stars as I crawl up towards a lone campfire on the mesa surrounded by skeletal remains

The lost headmistress for a one-room schoolhouse of swearing Mormon children, her skull still tied under a blue sunbonnet, stares up at the immobile night

Circus animals who escaped from the Great Western Show lie around the fire as if it were a waterhole, their carcasses stinking up the desert

A lazy swarm of nocturnal flies lifts and settles, lifts and settles, on the dead ex-governor of Nevada, last seen going outside for a cigar at The Territorial Ball

The hunted remains of deserters in stained sailor uniforms lie side by side at the edge of the firelight, still hiding from the ocean

Driven west by gunslinger novels and the desire to describe their quarters as rough hewn, two dead easterners have left their leg bones in cowboy boots

I panic and slide down the mesa to escape from this charnel campfire and ride away exhausted, galloping under a slow blaze of blue white starlight

My horse and I stumble through dead foothills and restless boulder fields, passing tumbleweed-filled homesteads trapped in the guano stench of a stale night

Unable to hold my head up, I slump back and forth until the animal just stops, so heavy with fatigue he sinks up to his hindquarters in the sand

A half-naked old man tracking his trousers, wakes us, claiming his cabin turned into swallow shadow at sunset and burrowed into a cliff edge

I shrug and put the spurs to my mount, driving him out of the sand, to head east— through a desert gray with algebraic indifference, hoping to find some sunrise

Natives point east and invent stories about golden cities in Quivira   Cracking the land as they cross, the Spaniards bear the image of a tortured Christ carved from memory and find Kansas:

Waitresses starting their cars in cafe parking lots, *For Sale* signs on rusting combines, silos full of rotting grain after the market fell through

Downhearted, the soldiers strangle their guides, discard their armor, and head back into the past, with crows offering encouragement as they drift sidelong against the wind

The men they left in Bernalillo have already retreated to Mexico Only a few old priests, misquoting the Bible and forgetting their hats in the snow are left to welcome them

Coronado limps back south with a headache   His pack animals are loaded with reports: Kansas is a land with the melody blown out of it, a grassland illustrating the wind and little more

As Francisco retreats towards the familiar skies of Mexico City, a drunk, walking home from El Madrid Bar, passes the clank and shuffle of the despondent conquistadors   Both parties pause and then move on, each regarding the other as wayward illusions

Coronado orders fresh troops, sent north to reinforce him, to turn back and writes in his journal: *There is nothing on the road into Quivira but week after week of solid moonlight and natives who leave you doubting everything you once believed*

85

Left alone for the next 50 years, the desert settles comfortably back into night

A one legged cowboy is hopping on the wooden dance floor trying to waltz with the town's new whore. Just a week ago, men were pounding old Hank on the back for bringing her to town.

But she never even asks their names. What kind of whore just dances? they ask each other. The women in town hate her fancy mail order dresses and the way she shows off the money she's taking from their men.

Finally the cowboys figure it out. This lousy whore doesn't think there's one of us good enough to fuck. She sits alone at the end of the bar for a week, without dancing, sipping on grenadine.

The men go back to grumbling over decks of bent up playing cards. Whipping out handguns. Sleeping drunk, with their heads on tables. Then just like that, she's moving on. Not a single man to see her off, with her fancy little hat pinned to the side of her head.

A line of the town's women in their plain bonnets, women with large forearms and not a shred of pity among them, watch the driver help her into the stagecoach. Alone inside, she rolls down her stockings and pulls off her wig with the little hat on it.

She lights a cigar. A man herself. Of course, the men in the bar all knew and so did all the men pretending to be women that they were married to, watching without expression as the stage leaves town.

1 Flies lie on the floor, dead after having spent the night on my face. I remember a handlebar mustache and a fancy vest— a 2-shot derringer in my chest, and the sound of my drunken voice coming from far away. I lean into the calaboose door and it opens, letting cool air surge in. In raw sunlight, a lone man is pounding stakes into the ground. I turn to go back inside, but the calaboose is full of shovels, picks, and surveying tools.

2 I take off for a slow train rolling around a bend in the Missouri. The surveyor yells for me to come back, as if something needs to be explained. The train pushes westward into night until a partially constructed western morning flashes past. Unplanted cactus lean against each other, next to piles of sand with shovels in them. Dray horses stand in puddles of their own shade near a dry riverbed. Their wagon bears a single word, written in simple lettering across its stained canvas:

W A T E R

3 Desert wildlife with Latin names written below them pass by on a long series of billboards. Shark fins move through the dunes, occasionally surfacing, teeth first, trying to gulp down skeletons of flightless birds as they migrate west. Beside the tracks, a young Navajo woman with two lambs under her right arm and a fierce child on her left, stare through the passing train. Behind her sits a small calaboose, ready for the trouble to start up again.

4   The freight car fills with other riders. Men in sheepskin chaps with stars embroidered on the sleeves of their gloves twirl their mustaches. Women in calico and buckskin fire rifles over their shoulders with a mirror in one hand, missing everything.   Their children let off long streams of cuss words and practice spitting into the landscape.   As we slow near the California coastline, I leap off, carrying a white door towards a blue house built out of cracker tins, bird nest plaster, and bottle crates.

5   An old man in a sleeping cap walks down the dusty boulevard followed by a swaybacked nag smiling broadly to show off her cheap set of dentures. Intermittently visible women twirl parasols along a bluff over the Pacific. Under a bright cloud held overhead by a guy-wire, auditions are being held for all roles. At dusk we sit together silently, in front of the darkened ocean, watching the flickering *raw cut* of the successful, heroic lives we hope to one day live.

Five men sit around a small blue campfire tucked in mountain snow. They have boiled their moccasins for food and wrapped blankets around their feet. They have eaten pine gum and beetles. They have hidden the murdered German, with strips of flesh cut from his thigh, out of sight.

Their eyes gleam with hatred at having been led to slow, frozen death by an imbecile. A man with his name misspelled in the tattoo on his arm. A Civil War veteran, discharged for epilepsy.

Afraid for his life, their guide sleeps with an axe clutched to his chest. Trapped in the deepening ultraviolet of snow falling into night, Alferd stands above them with the middle letters in his name rearranged. Eyes wide-open even though he is sound asleep. Axe raised over his head.

After 2 months, Alfred walks out alone. Well fed after so much time in the snow. Goes straight to the saloon at Saguache and starts drinking. His derangement betrayed by the five wallets he pulls money out of to pay for drinks.

An old man after his prison sentence for cannibalism, Alfred tries to write his memoir. The pen misbehaves, throwing in wrong letters. In each chapter, he cuts holes in lake ice for fish, but none come. The men he has led into the snow are trapped inside meat. In a winter constructed of dying campfires, Alfred stays alive by being alive.

Chasing him down snow covered train tracks in black and white, his long beard trailing, a murder of crows swoops down on me, allowing my enemy to disappear into the tree line

North of the border, the only trace I find of him is the rash of witnesses he's indoctrinated with his lies In Mexico, loaded on marijuana, villagers subvert my pursuit with stoned silences In the mountains, magpies carry away the bones of his latest meal to hide the evidence of his passing

I follow the prints of his bare feet through the dead western cities of the future Through the collapsed mirage of Las Vegas in 140 degree heat Past the remains of Albuquerque-- a few flickering street lights half buried in a dry river bed

We resurface in the 19th century-- as thunderclouds shower white doves into desert mountains I recognize his clothing on the branch of a submerged tree in the Colorado River and the line of bubbles he left as he swam away

*   *   *   *   *

We both marry and settle down on opposite sides of a town spilled into the yawn between mountain and snow covered frontier The city elders bar us from being in the same tavern, even if we are off-duty Despite my petition, the ransom of spouses is also prohibited

The law finds my enemy's remains in a valley of lilacs After they remove the meadow weeds growing among his vertebrae and report the skull as missing altogether, I am arrested and held over in the stockade

The day of my execution, the soldiers focus on the details of loading their rifles and take aim as the lieutenant raises his saber Before they can fire, my enemy, not dead at all, throws off his blanket and headdress and runs out the gate in a swirl of coyote yelps

The cavalry takes off in pursuit, with me in tow After a week, they tire of the chase, leaving me crossing swollen rivers and seeking high ground to spot him He waves up at me, ecstatic to be back in business, his eyes shining like clean windows with the desert behind them

He turned
towards   the night   and
talked about the desert   he'd
ridden through with Breton

The starving dogs
he'd seen digging up   graves
in burned out   adobe villages

The tumbleweeds
he'd shotgunned   as they
fled   without any wind to
blow them

And days   so
damned hot   the clouds
chewed off their own fur

He'd witnessed   a
barn   crossing a river   on
its own volition

And heard the
desert   circling   as it
complained of fish

Just this afternoon
he'd watched   a line of
buzzards   waiting on an
Overland Wagon   to see   if
a hanged man   would get
back in

And   we   just
listened   scarcely breathing

hoping he couldn't   tell   we
were staring   at   the
empty sockets   of his eyes

Our Brujo

We won't ever understand it; we won't ever unravel its secrets.
Thus we must treat the world as it is: a sheer mystery.
Carlos Casteneda

* * * * *

When we were still living in the past, a blue-eyed burro appeared. A dozen panting sparrows hopped behind him as he examined our dirt streets and mudbrick outhouses before disappearing. The next day the animal returned, carrying a man. Through the tangle of his beard, the brujo told us his mother had died before he was born. His grandmother had carried him to term in her ancient womb and since her withered breasts produced no milk, he was suckled by a herd of free-range goats.

He had survived in the desert by tracking the small owls that burrow for moisture. As proof, he produced two bota bags of sweet-water from before the biblical flood. He raised his arm and pointed a crooked finger towards the mountains where we had been hearing the sounds of dynamite for years as train crews tried to blast their way back to us. As if talking to savages, he told us that the crushed train cars in the ravine were proof of the failure of the Catholic gods and ridiculed our desire to be reunited with the rest of the world.

* * * * *

On our Saint's Day he produced a pulque from freshly chewed peyote buttons that gave us the ability to see our shoes through heavy tables. In the pulque's final stages we saw our fellow villagers with the heads of the dumb beasts they had been in their former lifetimes, an indelible image of the animal appetites that secretly controlled our village.

Every morning we listened to the explosions growing nearer, loud booms that toppled over the religious statues in our altars. The train crew knocked off for lunch each day at two and got too drunk to be around dynamite in the afternoon. In the silence, our brujo warned us that when the train returned it would replace our natural knowledge with the banality of modern science and unleash a plague of melancholy as the dreams of our youth became the memories of detached strangers.

* * * * *

A couple of weeks after the trains arrived, our brujo appeared shaved and nearly unrecognizable. He looked like any other old man in a cowboy hat with new boots. He announced he was going to Texas, stepped onto the evening train, and disappeared. When he left, we lost the ability to imagine anything we could not see before our eyes. Gone were our ancient legends about the cave where the wind hides its voice and our brujo's self-absorbed tale about the shambling old man with testicles the size of raisins, who repopulated desert villages after men lost their interest in sex.

A seedy side of town sprang up immediately after the trains arrived, giving rise to a group of railroad whores who preferred abandonment, viewing it as a sign of modernity, to the weak love of naïve, uncultured men. Years later, no one speaks of our brujo anymore and our children and grandchildren have left for the twin wonders of higher pay and complicated electronic devices. We survive on their allotments from the States, knowing that soon our village will revert to its natural condition of ruin, home only to wild burros that sniff around with their noses in the air, as if they too-- have become too good for our company.

* * * * *

Locked down in Deer Lodge for stabbing a Swede, I spent years imagining the wild scene inside the hotel he'd just left. Bald men suckled like infants on the laps of giantesses. A strong odor of opium wafted through the lobby. Women in masks with riding crops followed aroused young men upstairs. Love starved ranch hands and solitary miners shot at the moon as they waited on the veranda for their turn inside. My sordid fantasy ended each morning with the sound of the key unlocking my cell.

Just west of town, I killed my engine and rolled up on an abandoned, three-story Victorian sitting in an onion patch. All that was left of its furniture were scrape marks across a moonlit floor and a cold wood stove. A man-sized chunk was missing from the ballroom wallpaper as if a corpse finally freed itself from between the walls. As I walked back towards the road, the electricity in town went out, revealing a distant mountain of luminous snow flecked with campfires. I slept in the back seat of my car.

When I awoke, there was a blue square of paint on the second floor of the hotel, where somebody had pried a sign off the weathered wood. I could see the dirt trampled in the former flower beds by hundreds of pairs of shoes sneaking up to the windows at night. An old woman opened the front door, saw my car, and slowly retreated back into the Blue Hotel. As she closed the drapes on the second floor, I drove away, embarrassed to be part of the intruding force that besieged her each night. Despite the odds against it, I spent the day hopeful that we'd grow old together. In the quiet hours, before the turnkey unlocks my cell.

The sentry shoulders a Springfield flintlock, like a tonsured monk guarding a registry of all the evil I is capable of. I looks like a mustache on its way west. I sings like starlings in a sycamore tree after a late snow. I sweats like a Spaniard pushing a cart with square wheels towards El Paso. I is from the future with a plume of train smoke steaming over his shoulder. I will be an old man by the time I is born along the old Missouri.

All the men in town wake up to a ringing phone, but it's nothing, not even a picture of a phone. They get up in buckskin trousers, boots, and out of focus beards—eager to try out their hanging skills in Shiloh. As they thunder towards Wyoming, I is riding a giant snake into town, missing one finger wearing cologne. Despite his many mutilations, the town's women are in front of mirrors, powdering under their breasts, flush with desire, as they tremulously wait for I to arrive.

                              Outside the train
a tableau of western   silences
enforced by passenger car windows:
                              Sleeping cattle
silently shift   their weight   from one
foot   to another
                              The dust
plume   of a horseman
noiselessly gallops   ten miles off
                              Lightning cracks
over hills   covered with burnt scrub
oak
                              The distant
image   of an Apache astride his
pony   articulates the silence
of a blue mesa

                                        A
nervous easterner   on his first trip
west   disembarks   in the shadow
of a water tank
                              Three men
watch him stumble   gripsack   in
hand   down the steps   of a Pullman
Car
                              Howdy, Judge
Henry send you to take me to the ranch? he
nervously   asks   the   silent   strangers
outside the depot
                              A rail
thin cowboy   winces slightly   and
opens his mouth   as if to speak
                              As a black
swarm   engulfs   the traveler leaving a
shimmering pile   of dust where   he
once stood

100

                                        On cue
the wind picks up   clearing the station
platform   &   reimposing   the
patient image of
                                    Three men
leaning back   each with one boot
against the depot wall   as   the train
vanishes   from sight

A two-bit thief caught climbing out a
dry goods store window is dragged
at the end of a lasso into the desert
and left for dead,   still clutching a
box of stolen matches, as wild dogs
try to pull off his boots

A
few minutes after midnight, the
scarred thief lights a stolen cigar and
blows a long stream of smoke   into
the cool night air, with the screams of
horses trapped in the burning livery
stable behind him

The morning sun rises behind the
posse as it boils out of town, a furious
blur of men kicking their heels and
horses   with   frothing   mouths
arrowing across the alkali

Twenty
miles in the opposite direction, and
hidden in the shade of a boulder
escarpment, the arsonist is reading a
dime western

Licking
his thumb, he turns the pages of *The
Helltown   Gunslinger*,   imagining
himself a great shootist,   dumb
with luck, stopping at the edge of a
sinister town, its windows bristling
with rifles

I search a line of vegetation dying in the desert along a wide river too stingy to share its water with the trees. An old wrangler rides his horse down to the river and lets it drink. I slip into the brush, just as a breeze rattles through, waving the wanted posters, dozens of different outlaws nailed to trees. The old timer pulls the horse's head up and trick walks him backwards, refilling hoof prints back to the tree line.

Not a minute later, a posse boils up to the edge of the river. They spot his tracks and spur their animals into the water. The old wrangler rides his mount back to the water's edge. The men chasing him sweep downstream until the final deputy goes under — with a raised arm making an obscene hand gesture.

"Something I learned while I was here in the cavalry," he says. "I saw an Apache fire a round into the air from the other side of the river. Our gold haired colonel drew his sidearm and charged into the water. Never saw him again. Apache laughed so damn hard he fell from his pony and began dry humping the sand. The Rio de los Rios never turns loose of what it swallows."

Since he's talkin' to me, I step out of cover. He has an empty eye socket in the middle of a long knife scar. He's wearing two white necklaces of human teeth with their roots still attached. There's a leather handled quirt made out of braided human hair hanging from his saddle horn. He leans on his pommel and says, "Smile real pretty would you? Any gold in your mouth?"

I smile to show my stained brown teeth, half rotted from chewing tobacco when I was a kid. "You seen an old paint while you was riding up? He spooked last night. Thought he might have headed for water," I ask.

"You're a sorry excuse for a horseman, ain't you? A poor dumb sumbitch that gave up on bathin' or taking down his drawers to piss. I don't blame your horse for partin' ways with ye," he says, shakin' his head. "Look up river about a quarter mile."

He sniffs the air and licks his finger. Points at a thick puff of slow cloud moving west, across the desert. "We'll have to continue our conversation some other time," he says and spurs his horse. They leave a trail of dust for half a mile. Pick up the shade of the cloud and slow to a walk. Like an old lady crossing a sunny street under a parasol.

I find my horse up river. Crackin around in the brush, trapped with one hoof on his reins. Trying to yank his head up to get away from me. I kick my nag in the ribs. Yank the rein out from under his hoof and drag him behind me. A pair of dumb, stinkin' sumbitches strugglin' through sunlight. Hopin' to get back to Fortuna with their teeth still in their heads.

The town stands
exposed in raw sunlight
as a bullet hurries
towards it

A flash of
light enters the bank
clerk's body releasing a
pink mist into the air

His
bloody
shirt gets investigated by
flies as pieces of a lead
slug drop from forceps
into a steel pan

The
surgeon's tobacco smoke
turns blue over the
operating table

While
outside, the wind has
picked up, pelting the
windows with dirt and
small rocks

In the
waiting room, the teller's
relatives spit and let on
that

Although the
weather is prone to
gunfire, not a one of them
would live anywhere else

A man with a shrunken head, wearing a cavalry boot for a hat, rides on the lead wagon's perch, guiding the misshapen performers out of the desert. Families stream towards the center of town in Sunday clothes, as if a biblical event has just arrived in the form of a carnival.

Sitting like a chess piece on a stool, a legless woman sings an aria about the infinite wonder inside the tent. A quarter dollar to see a fish skeleton with a small human skull, in a jar of cloudy formaldehyde. Another quarter to see a bald woman with webbed feet sitting on an ostrich egg in a padded nest.

A pair of shoes walks by themselves around center ring, using the voice of William Jennings Bryant to insult the audience with courtroom eloquence. Hours later, an enraged posse, determined to shoot the black oxfords full of holes, is halted by bone darkness, as the shadow of an engorged moon falls across the lunar landscape of the western desert.

Up through the black air, the distant lanterns of the carnival wagons can be seen heading towards the Sea of Tranquility. The lathered posse gazes up, listening to the microcephalic at the reins whistling a mournful Chinese tune, unaware he made a wrong turn on the way down to Yuma Crossing. In the steam rising off their horses, the cowboys sit dejected. Having failed to put an end to this insurrection of shoe leather, they fear that their own boots will soon turn against them.

(1)

A wild eyed pony appeared out of the darkness with a white handprint painted on his rump. He wanted to herd with our horses but wouldn't let us near him to unhitch the fancy saddle he was dragging around. We sat by the fire stoned. Trying to figure whether his rider was eaten by coyotes or a starved prospector and about the Indian he must've killed to steal that horse. We shooed the pony off to get some sleep and lay in our bedrolls, listening to the rockslides he started as he dragged his way up the hill. I was deep into sleep when that damned animal screamed so loud, cones fell out of the pine. Jeb and I jumped up and nearly shot each other. The pony just wanted us to see him up there, on the ridgeline, all shining in raw moonlight.

(2)

The next night an old man woke us, wearing a get-up of rabbit skins stitched together off the desert floor. Asked if we'd seen his ride. "He thought I was dead this time. Pawed the ground all around me and then took off. He's an idealist. The world just isn't good enough for such a horse. And brothers, you should move away from these malpais. They are crawling with horned vipers and toads that shoot venom from their eyes. This is indeed an evil place," he said, stepping up next to the campfire. A dead sidewinder dangled from each hand. We waved our hands in front of his face. He was blind as an Old Testament prophet living on wild honey and locust. "How'd you find us?" I asked. "I could hear you snoring from miles away," he said.

(3)

Sudden as a meteor streaking overhead, he took his leave, clearing a path through the night's reptiles with the never-ending pile of talk booming out of him. He tracked up the hill, listening for the holes his pony left in last night's silence. We just sat there beside the campfire, like two pieces of punctuation with the words removed between them. Next morning, the ground around our tethers was covered with snakes the horses had stomped to death. We lit out, dodging posse, into open terrain baked clean by the sun and hid in loose rock, north of the mail routes, in earthquake country. We kept our fire low, so low not even a blind man could find us. And barely spoke, hoping not to attract any more strangers who didn't know we weren't dead yet. Much less the others, sick with vengeance and reward posters, who wished we were.

Since we been out west I've been snakebit twice. Jeb got himself chased down an arroyo by a flashflood even though it hadn't rained in two weeks.

And we both got chewed up in our bedrolls by a low cloud of freetail bats.

That was before we figured out as long as you stay stoned everything backs off and leaves you alone.

So, we're smokin' dope in the bosque and listening to the door of an abandoned church slamming shut up on the hill, even though there's no wind.

Finally, a cool stream of river air cuts through the warm evening. "You feel that?"   Jeb asks. "Yeah, it's like time stopped moving for a few seconds," I say.

But then there's a voice. **"Put your hands in the air!"** Some law-crazed white man is sittin' on the biggest palomino I ever seen and looking down his rifle at me.

I don't say nothin'. If he ain't real, he should go away in a couple seconds.

He fires a shot up in the air to get our attention and the bullet knocks a hornet's nest out of a cottonwood.

His horse knows what's coming and takes off running to get the fuck away from him.

Hornets chase the lawman splashing out into the river and send him bubbling downstream. Jeb walks over and picks up the rifle.

"How'd he ever make it **this far**? That's what I'd like to know," he asks, as I take a big hit, hold it, and pass him the joint.

After a morning spent as dark blots. Rising on thermals in a dry blue sky. The buzzards return to pace on the roof.

Of the abandoned mission. Watching a funeral procession. Leaving the newer church. Followed by a starving dog.

Who the next morning is himself buried. Under the black wings of buzzards. Who re-ascend to the roof of the church.

Above a pair of unlatched doors. Banging themselves from their hinges. Below a broken round window.

Exhaling a stream of bats each night. Like a smoker relapsing. Into the grip of a nocturnal habit.

One of the desert's addictions. Like burying old churches. With waves of fine sand. Until all that is visible. Is a solitary bell tower.

A partial memory of a church. Eroded by senile dementia. Hardly a church at all. Just a bell tower paced by buzzards.

Watching a distant highway. Occasionally visible through swirls of sand. A highway where the blessings of probability. Play out in a word.

Written in rabbit fur. A word. Dried out on asphalt. A word. Written in the marrow of buzzards. A word. Scrutinized with Talmudic intensity.

Dead.

1. At dusk, a pinch cheeked man of the cloth rode into town behind a pair of exhausted horses, propped up a cheap slab of white marble with the name **Joe Black** carved on it, and stood an empty coffin on its end. Swifts played in the air as he paused to look towards the distant peaks. "No man can resist the coffin in which they'll be buried nor the stone that will set on their grave, not even Joe Black!"

A boy, mocking the preacher, did a vulture hop behind him and was suddenly circled by a spray of lightning quick gunfire. The preacher's pistol back in its holster before anyone could draw a full breath. At dusk, he stuck two poles into the ground with kerosene torches atop them, so the coffin was visible to the distant darkness.

At midnight, he extinguished his torches, and rode straight of town, singing an ancient Coptic hymn. His wagon, occasionally visible under the dry, lightning infested sky, slowly crossed the desert towards morning. Two days later, Joe Black showed up, bedraggled by dirt, looking for water.

2. "He said you'd follow your coffin, the way a dog follows a scent." I told him. "That's just bad poetry," Joe Black replied. "This preacher robs fresh graves. Certainly you noticed an odor about the clothes he wears. He's also a black hearted horse thief. Those are _my_ animals that drag him from town to town." Unwilling to betray a man of the cloth, we looked guiltily at each other, and pointed north.

Joe Black's footsteps, one after the next, spurted up a flourlike gray dust as he trod off into the distance, headed the wrong way. We were certain one of them was a dead man. Some said, preacher made a better corpse. Others, that Mr. Black smelled like graveyard dirt. We all agreed that we weren't long to follow if it didn't rain.

Soon after, we packed up wagons and rode out, passing the broken steeple of our little chapel, a field of waist high dead grass with an abandoned harrow, and our dead fruit trees lined up in the afternoon heat. We finally overtook the clouds that always gathered on the horizon, unable to rain, and passed into history. Without a backward glance, we left our town— built at the boundary between the living and the dead, buried in the Nevada wind, a mystery for someone else to claim.

The wind turns pages of a pulp
western left on the patio, as if
considering whether it's worth
finishing. . . The jailer is leaning back
in his chair, his gun belt hanging on a
dowel behind him. His nap facilitates
the Kid's escape, right before the
book suddenly flips 30 pages
forward in the wind. The Kid climbs
out the saloon window, slides down the slanted roof and stumbles
off into the desert. The woman he leaves behind cracks open the
door so the sheriff can see she's alone. Blown 87 pages further on,
the Kid is rescued by a Winchester bullet that severs the hanging
rope. The townspeople run from rifle fire as he escapes in a
stampede of horses, riding sideways. The Kid flips to his lowest
point, twenty pages from the beginning of his story, in the moment
that forever turned him against the law, falsely accused and beaten
with a bullwhip.

My own life halts and races forward like someone else's story. Most
days feel like I'm stumbling out into a dirt avenue towards a man
who knows how to use the pistol in his belt. Assured of failure, I'm
surprised to see the streets are lined with my family members,
living and dead, standing in the shade along closed storefronts.
Unlike the Kid, I have a life off the page, in a world of mown lawns
where you only get to kill one person so you've got to choose
carefully. In the backyard, a copy of The Helltown Gunslinger
furiously whips back and forth. A few clouds drift over, disinterest-
ed in the desert vegetation. A pair of
mourning doves scratches around
behind the swamp cooler, looking for
shelter from the coming storm. As I
bring the book into my house, I realize
that, like the Kid, I also have learned
to identify with the events in my life,
but only belatedly.

Acknowledgements

My thanks to the publications in which these poems have previously appeared:

"Woman Submerged in a Car": *AGNI (online)*
"Frenchette" *and* "Message for the Fotomat": *Blue Mesa Review*
 "Along the Pacific Coast Highway" and "The Last Days before the Age of Industry": *Double Room*
"Short Hand": Bartlett, Lee, VB Price and Dianne Edenfield Edwards, eds., *In Company, An Anthology of New Mexico Poets after 1960*, 2004, University of New Mexico Press,
 "Ranch Surrealism,": *Ninth Letter*
"Budapest: A Labyrinth" and "Three Christmas Still Lifes": *Outlaw Poetry*
"Sleeping Sickness": *Sentence*
"The Stare of Drowned Statuary": *Willow Springs*

Biography

Lawrence Goeckel is a former master sergeant who served in Korea, Kosovo, Spain, Turkey, the Philippines and Iraq as an electronics warfare and aircraft technician. After retiring from the Air Force in 2005, he completed his Masters in Fine Arts on the GI Bill at the University of New Mexico (UNM). He taught at UNM and was the poetry editor for *Blue Mesa Review*. Goeckel was a longtime poker buddy and poetry compatriot of Gene Frumkin. He was teaching English at Eldorado High School in Albuquerque, NM when he suffered a series of strokes that cut short his writing career.

In the Spring 2007 issue of *Double Room*, Goeckel wrote about his work: Russell Edson, who I admire very much, makes a useful distinction between fiction and poetry in Double Room #4, claiming that: "Fiction describes reality with words, poetry with images." He goes on to claim that poetry is not a language art the way that fiction is; since poetry works with images, it is closer to painting or silent film. The successful prose poem thereby utilizes the strengths of prose and poetry, art and cinema, and by so doing, hopefully succeeds in tripping up the reading public, landing them face first in a poem without them knowing it. To engender this confusion, I present my prose poems fully justified, or in a strip down the middle of the page— like a photocopy of a newspaper article. I like to think of my prose poems as statues that have been reassembled into blocks of marble, with their potentiality still visible.

The text of these poems is written in Book Antiqua.

According to Webtype, most typefaces are more chiseled and aggressively geometric in their countenance than Book Antiqua. Imagine instead the veiled face of a Venetian Renaissance woman who gently inks an occasional verse in her orchard or signs a visiting card to a long-lost cousin recently returned home from an arduous journey to the West with sand in his shoes.

Book Design by Stefi Weisburd

More praise for The Longing of the Optic Nerve

Reading Goeckel's poetry is like eating a fine aged steak cooked rare over a wood fire. Each poem has its own special flavor that explodes in nuance, surprising images, and connections that you may not have noticed but clearly make sense as you digest them. Some of them stick in your teeth and you find yourself seeing the images again as you look out the window, yet there's music that is understated, filling your ear with a melody you didn't know you knew, but you do. Take in these poems slowly, let them work their way into your system as if they are a rare expensive meal cooked to perfection.

— Don McIver Sunday Chatter's Poetry Wrangler, KUNM Freeform DJ, and editor of *A Bigger Boat: the Unlikely Success of the Albuquerque Slam Scene* (UNM Press)

Larry Goeckel's compelling poetry startles at every turn and resonates. His work has a deep sense of place woven with threads of film noir to turn the ordinary into the extraordinary. Goeckel's surreal vision captures a unique angle on the world."

— Diane Thiel, author *Echolocations, Resistance Fantasies*

"Larry Goeckel's poetry explores a variety of registers that blur the line between poetry & prose. He narrates in a way that both plays with & advances a hard-edged lyricism of the American West, surprising at each turn."

— John Tritica, author *Sound Remains*, co-founder, of L)Edge, a poetry circle

Larry Goeckel's writing ranges from harsh surrealism to storytelling turned upon itself in places disparate as Kosovo, Hungary, New Mexico and places unknown. The writer's voice can be a gunslinger, detective, shaman, soldier, dreamer stuck here on earth in flesh and blood. Poems/stories/sketches appear sometimes in columnar newspaper form so you may be reading the jarring news or a narrative carefully spilling down the page. There's a René Magritte-Edward Hopper visual jigsaw with voices of French Surrealist Poets bemused by Gene Frumkin and Ed Dorn and presented uniquely by the tale teller. It's an appreciated freshness that the author presents, as troubling as the world is.

—Larry Goodell, author *Here on Earth*, founder Duende Press

Among the growing postulates of lunar geometry, / hunger is the space between objects," writes Lawrence Goeckel in his *tour de force*, *The Longing of the Optic Nerve*. In these remarkable poems, Goeckel's speaker hungers for connection in a world pockmarked by "bearded fish," "Human / silhouettes with animal heads," and "A pair of shoes [that] walks by themselves around center ring, using the voice of William Jennings Bryant to insult the audience." Goeckel finds connection in dissonances, discovering a poetics that is visionary in its very *resistance to* "vision." These poems are short films, parables, paintings, hallucinatory bedtime stories— cosmic and earthly. They invoke Surrealism yet embrace the anti-poem, as if Benjamin Péret and Nicanor Parra prepared a dinner of gesso and paint thinner to entice Chagall to invite them to pose with one of his circus ponies and a man with a green face. "'The truly crazy are always the calmest,'" Goeckel says, proffering a crazy wisdom at the core of these poems. Larry Goeckel has written an enormously profound and invigorating book, giving us a world aslant that is remarkably steadfast, generous, and generative.

—George Kalamaras, Poet Laureate of Indiana (2014-2016)